Tertullian
Scorpiace

Tertullian
Scorpiace

Tertullian
Scorpiace

© Lighthouse Publishing 2018

All rights reserved. Without limiting the rights under copyright reserved above, no part of this publication may be reproduced, stored in a retrieval system, or transmitted, in any form or by any means (electronic, mechanical, photocopying, recording or otherwise), without the prior written permission of the copyright owner of this book.

Published by
Lighthouse Christian Publishing
SAN 257-4330
5531 Dufferin Drive
Savage, Minnesota, 55378
United States of America

www.lighthousechristianpublishing.com

Tertullian

Introductory Note.

The Second Class of Tertullian's works, according to the logical method I have endeavored to carry out, is that which includes his treatises against the heresies of his times. In these, the genius of our author is brilliantly illustrated, while, in melancholy fact, he is demonstrating the folly of his own final lapse and the wickedness of that schism and heresy into which he fell away from Truth. Were it not that history abounds in like examples of the frailty of the human intellect and of the insufficiency of "man that walketh to direct his steps," we should be forced to a theory of mental decay to account for inconsistencies so gross and for delusions so besotted. "Genius to madness is *indeed* allied," and who knows but something like that imbecility which closed the career of Swift may have been the fate of this splendid wit and versatile man of parts? Charity, admiration and love force this inquiry upon my own mind continually, as I explore his fascinating pages. And the order in which the student will find them in this series, will lead, I think, to similar reflections on the part of many readers. We observe a natural bent and turn of mind, even in his Catholic writings, which indicate his perils. These are more and more apparent in his recent works, as his enthusiasm heats itself into a frenzy which at last becomes a rage. He breaks down by degrees, as in orthodoxy so also in force and in character. It is almost like the collapse of Solomon or of Bacon. And though our own times have produced no example of stars of equal magnitude, to become falling-stars, we have seen illustrations the most humiliating, of those calm words of Bishop Kaye: "Human nature often presents the curious phenomenon of a union of the most opposite qualities in the same mind; of vigor, acuteness and discrimination on some subjects, with imbecility, dullness and bigotry on others." Milton, himself another example of his own threnode, breaks forth in this splendid utterance of lyrical confession:

> "God of our fathers what is man?
>   Nor do I name of men the common rout,
>   That, wandering loose about,
> Grow up and perish as the summer fly,
> Heads without name, no more remembered,
> But such as thou hast solemnly elected,
> With gifts and graces eminently adorned,
> To some great work, thy glory
>   And people's safety, *which in part they effect.*"

And here, I must venture a remark on the ambiguity of the expressions concerning our author's Montanism. In the treatise against Marcion, written late in his career, Tertullian identifies himself with the Church and strenuously defends its faith and its apostolic order. In only rare instances does his weakness for the "new prophecy" crop out, and then, it is only as one identifies himself with a school within the church. Precisely so Fenelon maintained his milder Montanism, without a thought of deserting the Latin Church. Afterwards Fenelon drew back, but at last poor Tertullian fell away. So with the Jansenists. They credited the *miracles* and the *convulsions* (or ecstasies) of their school, and condemned those who rejected them, as Tertullian condemns the *Psychics*. The great expounder of the Nicene Faith (Bp. Bull) does indeed speak very decidedly of Tertullian as a *lapser*, even when he wrote his first book against Marcion. His semi-schismatic position must be allowed. But, was it a *formal* lapse at that time? The English non-jurors were long in communion with the Church, even while they denounced their brethren and the "Erastianizing" clergy, much as Tertullian does the *Psychics*. St. Augustine speaks of *Tertullianists* with great moderation, and notes the final downfall of our author as something distinct from Tertullianism. When we reflect, therefore, that only four of all his varied writings (now extant) are proofs of an accomplished lapse, ought we not carefully to maintain the distinction between the Montanistic Tertullian and Tertullian the Montanist? Bishop Bull, it seems to me would not object to this way of putting it, when we consider his own discrimination in the following weighty words. He says:

"A clear distinction must be made between those works which Tertullian, when already a Montanist, wrote specifically in defense of Montanism *against the church*, and those which he composed, as a Montanist indeed, yet *not in defense of Montanism against the church*, but rather, *in defense of the common doctrines of the church*—and of Montanus, in opposition to other heretics."

Now in arranging the works of this second class, *the Prescription* comes logically first, because, written in Orthodoxy, it forcibly upholds the Scriptural Rule of Faith, the Catholic touchstone of all professed verity. It is also a necessary Introduction to the great work against Marcion which I have placed next in order; giving it the precedence to which it is entitled in part on chronological ground, in part because of the general purity of its material with the exhibition it presents of the author's mental processes and of his very gradual decline from Truth.

Very fortunate were the Edinburgh Editors in securing for this work and some others, the valuable labors of Dr. Holmes, of whom I have elsewhere given some biographical particulars. The merit and fullness of his annotations are so marked, that I have been spared a great deal of work, such as I was forced to bestow on the former volumes of this American Edition. But on the other hand these pages have given me much patient study and toil as an editor, because of the "shreds and patches" in which Tertullian comes to us, in the Edinburgh Series; and because of some typographical peculiarities, exceptional in that Series itself, and presenting complications, when transferred to a new form of mechanical arrangement.

For example, apart from some valuable material which belongs to the General Preface, and which I have transferred accordingly, the following dislocations confronted me to begin with: The *Marcion* is presented to us in Volume VII. apart from the other writings of Tertullian. At the close of Vol. XI. we reach the *Ad Nationes*, of which Dr. Holmes is the translator, another hand (Mr. Thelwall's) having been employed on former pages of that volume. It is not till we reach Volume XV. that Tertullian again appears, but this volume is wholly the work of Dr. Holmes. Finally, in Volume XVIII., we meet Tertullian again, (Mr. Thelwall the able translator), but, here is placed the "Introduction" to all the works of

Tertullian, which, of course, I have, transferred to its proper place. I make these explanations by no means censoriously, but to point out at once the nature of my own task, and the advantage that accrues to the reader, by the order in which the works of the great Tertullian appear in this edition, enabling him to compare different or parallel passages, all methodically arranged in consecutive pages, without a minute's search, or delay.

Now, as to typographical difficulties to which I have referred, Dr. Holmes marks all his multiplied and useful notes with *brackets*, which are almost always superfluous, and which in this American Edition are used to designate my own contributions, when printed with the text, or apart from Preface and Elucidations. These, therefore, I have removed necessarily and with no appreciable loss to the work, but great gain to the beauty of the page. But, again, Dr. Holmes' translations are all so heavily bracketed as to become an eyesore, and the disfigured pages have been often complained of as afflictive to the reader. Many words strictly implied by the original Latin, and which should therefore be unmarked, are yet put between brackets. Even minute words (*and*, or *to wit*, or *again*,) when, in the nature of the case the English idiom requires them, are thus marked. I have not retained these blemishes; but when an inconsiderable word or a repetition does add to the sense, or qualify it, I have italicized such words, throwing more important interpolations into parenthetical marks, which are less painful to the sight than brackets. I have found them quite as serviceable to denote the auxiliary word or phrase; and where the author himself uses a parenthesis, I have observed very few instances in which a sensible reader would confound it with the translator's efforts to eke out the sense. Sometimes, an awkward interpolation has been thrown into a footnote.

Occasionally the crabbed sentences of the great Carthaginian are so obscure that Dr. Holmes has been unable to make them lucid, although, with the original in hand, he probably felt a force in his own rendering which the mere English reader must fail to perceive. In a few such instances, noting the fact in the margin, I have tried to bring out the sense, by slight modifications of punctuation and arrangement. Occasionally too I have dropped a superfluous interpolation (such as *e.g.*, *to conclude*, or let me say again,) when I have found that it only served to clog and overcharge a sentence. Last of all, Dr. Holmes' *headings* have sometimes been condensed, to avoid phrases and sentences immediately recurring in the chapter. These purely mechanical parts require a terse form of statement, like those in the English Bible, and I have frequently reduced them on that model, dropping redundant adverbs and adjectives to bring out the catchwords.

Scorpiace.

Antidote for the Scorpion's Sting.

Chapter I.

The earth brings forth, as if by suppuration, great evil from the diminutive scorpion. The poisons are as many as are the kinds of it, the disasters as many as are also the species of it, the pains as many as are also the colors of it. Nicander writes on the subject of scorpions, and depicts them. And yet to smite with the tail—which tail will be whatever is prolonged from the hindmost part of the body, and scourges—is the one movement which they all use when making an assault. Wherefore that succession of knots in the scorpion, which in the inside is a thin poisoned veinlet, rising up with a bow-like bound, draws tight a barbed sting at the end, after the manner of an engine for shooting missiles. From which circumstance they also call after the scorpion, the warlike implement which, by its being drawn back, gives an impetus to the arrows. The point in their case is also a duct of extreme minuteness, to inflict the wound; and where it penetrates, it pours out poison. The usual time of danger is the summer season: fierceness hoists the sail when the wind is from the south and the southwest. Among cures, certain substances supplied by nature have very great efficacy; magic also puts on some bandage; the art of healing counteracts with lancet and cup. For some, making haste, take also beforehand a protecting draught; but sexual intercourse drains it off, and they are dry again. We have faith for a defense, if we are not smitten with distrust itself also, in immediately making the sign and adjuring, and besmearing the heel with the beast. Finally, we often aid in this way even the heathen, seeing we have been endowed by God with that power which the apostle first used when he despised the viper's bite. What, then, does this pen of yours offer, if faith is safe by what it has of its own? That it may be safe by what it has of its own also at other times, when it is subjected to scorpions of its own. These, too, have a troublesome littleness, and are of different sorts, and are armed in one manner, and are stirred up at a definite time, and that not another than one of burning heat. This among Christians is a season of persecution. When, therefore, faith is greatly agitated, and the Church burning, as represented by the bush, then the Gnostics break out, then the Valentinians creep forth, then all the opponents of martyrdom bubble up, being themselves also hot to strike, penetrate, kill. For, because they know that many are artless and also inexperienced, and weak moreover, that a very great number in truth are Christians who veer about with the wind and conform to its moods, they perceive that they are never to be approached more than when fear has opened the entrances to the soul, especially when some display of ferocity has already arrayed with a crown the faith of martyrs. Therefore, drawing along the tail hitherto, they first of all apply it to the feelings, or whip with it as if on empty space. Innocent persons undergo such suffering. So that you may suppose the speaker to be a brother or a heathen of the better sort. A sect troublesome to nobody so dealt with! Then they pierce. Men are perishing without a reason. For that they are perishing, and without a reason, is the first insertion. Then they now strike mortally. But the unsophisticated souls know not what is written, and what meaning it bears, where and when and before whom we must confess, or ought, save that this, to die for God, is, since He preserves me, not even artlessness, but folly, nay madness. If He kills me, how will it be His duty to preserve me? Once for all Christ died for us, once for all He was slain that we might not be slain. If He demands the like from me in return, does He also look for salvation from my death by violence? Or does God importune for the blood of men, especially if He refuses that of bulls and he-goats? Assuredly He had rather have the repentance than the death of the sinner. And how is He eager for the death of those who are not sinners? Whom will not these, and perhaps other subtle devices containing heretical poisons, pierce either for doubt if not for destruction, or for irritation if not for death? As for you, therefore, do you, if faith is on the alert, smite on the spot the scorpion with a curse, so far as you can, with your sandal, and leave it dying in its own stupefaction? But if it gluts the wound, it drives the poison inwards, and makes it hasten into the bowels; forthwith all the former senses become dull, the blood of the mind freezes, the flesh of the spirit pines away, loathing for the Christian name is accompanied by a sense of sourness. Already the understanding also seeks for itself a place where it may throw up; and thus, once for all, the weakness with which it has been smitten breathes out wounded faith either in heresy or in heathenism. And now the present state of matters is such, that we are in the midst of an intense heat, the very dog-star of persecution—a state originating doubtless with the dog-headed one himself. Of some Christians the fire, of others the sword, of others the beasts, have made trial; others are hungering in prison for the martyrdoms of which they have had a taste in the meantime by being subjected to clubs and claws besides. We ourselves, having been appointed for pursuit, are like hares being hemmed in from a distance; and heretics go about according to their wont. Therefore, the state of the times has prompted me to prepare by my pen, in opposition to the little beasts which trouble our sect, our antidote against poison, that I may thereby effect cures. You who read will at the same time drink. Nor is the draught bitter. If the utterances of the Lord are sweeter than honey and the honeycombs, the juices are from that source. If the promise of God flows with milk and honey, the ingredients which go to make that draught have the smack of this. "But woe to them who turn sweet into bitter, and light into darkness." For, in like manner, they also who oppose martyrdoms, representing salvation to be destruction, transmute sweet into bitter, as well as light into darkness; and thus, by preferring this very wretched life to that most blessed one, they put bitter for sweet, as well as darkness for light.

Chapter II.

But not yet about the good to be got from martyrdom must we learn, without our having first heard about the duty of suffering it; nor must we learn the usefulness of it, before we have heard about the necessity for it. The (question of the) divine warrant goes first—whether God has willed and also commanded ought of the kind, so that they who assert that it is not good are not plied with arguments for thinking it profitable save when they have been subdued. It is proper that heretics be driven to duty, not enticed. Obstinacy must be conquered, not coaxed. And, certainly, that will be pronounced beforehand quite good enough, which will be shown to have been instituted and also enjoined by God. Let the Gospels wait a little, while I set forth their root the Law, while I ascertain the will of God from those writings from which I recall to mind Himself also: "I am," says He, "God, thy God, who have brought thee out of the land of Egypt. Thou shalt have no other gods besides me. Thou shalt not make unto thee a likeness of those things which are in heaven, and which are in the earth beneath, and which are in the sea under the earth. Thou shalt not worship them, nor serve them. For I am the Lord thy God." Likewise, in the same book of Exodus: "Ye yourselves have seen that I have talked with you from heaven. Ye shall not make unto you gods of silver, neither shall ye make unto you gods of gold." To the following effect also, in Deuteronomy: "Hear, O Israel; The Lord thy God is one: and thou shalt love the Lord thy God with all thy heart and all thy might, and with all thy soul." And again: "Neither do thou forget the Lord thy God, who brought thee forth from the land of Egypt, out of the house of bondage. Thou shalt fear the Lord thy God, and serve Him only, and cleave to Him, and swear by His name. Ye shall not go after strange gods, and the gods of the nations which are around about you, because the Lord thy God is also a jealous God among you, and lest His anger should be kindled against thee, and destroy thee from off the face of the earth." But setting before them blessings and curses, He also says: "Blessings shall be yours, if ye obey the commandments of the Lord your God, whatsoever I command you this day, and do not wander from the way which I have commanded you, to go and serve other gods whom ye know not." And as to rooting them out in every way: "Ye shall utterly destroy all the places wherein the nations, which ye shall possess by inheritance, served their gods, upon mountains and hills, and under shady trees. Ye shall overthrow all their altars, ye shall overturn and break in pieces their pillars, and cut down their groves, and burn with fire the graven images of the gods themselves, and destroy the names of them out of that place." He further urges, when they (the Israelites) had entered the land of promise, and driven out its nations: "Take heed to thy self, that thou do not follow them after they be driven out from before thee, that thou do not inquire after their gods, saying, As the nations serve their gods, so let me do likewise." But also says He: "If there arise among you a prophet himself, or a dreamer of dreams, and giveth thee a sign or a wonder, and it come to pass, and he say, Let us go and serve other gods, whom ye know not, do not hearken to the words of that prophet or dreamer, for the Lord your God proveth you, to know whether ye fear God with all your heart and with all your soul. After the Lord your God ye shall go, and fear Him, and keep His commandments, and obey His voice, and serve Him, and cleave unto Him. But that prophet or dreamer shall die; for he has spoken to turn thee away from the Lord thy God." But also in another section, "If, however, thy brother, the son of thy father or of thy mother, or thy son, or thy daughter, or the wife of thy bosom, or thy friend who is as thine own soul, solicit thee, saying secretly, let us go and serve other gods, which thou knowest not, nor did thy fathers, of the gods of the nations which are round about thee, very nigh unto thee or far off from thee, do not consent to go with him, and do not hearken to him. Thine eye shall not spare him, neither shalt thou pity, neither shalt thou preserve him; thou shalt certainly inform upon him. Thine hand shall be first upon him to kill him, and afterwards the hand of thy people; and ye shall stone him, and he shall die, seeing he has sought to turn thee away from the Lord thy God." He adds likewise concerning cities, that if it appeared that one of these had, through the advice of unrighteous men, passed over to other gods, all its inhabitants should be slain, and everything belonging to it become accursed, and all the spoil of it be gathered together into all its places of egress, and be, even with all the people, burned with fire in all its streets in the sight of the Lord God; and, says He, "it shall not be for dwelling in forever: it shall not be built again any more, and there shall cleave to thy hands naught of its accursed plunder, that the Lord may turn from the fierceness of His anger." He has, from His abhorrence of idols, framed a series of curses too: "Cursed be the man who maketh a graven or a molten image, an abomination, the work of the hands of the craftsman, and putteth it in a secret place." But in Leviticus He says: "Go not ye after idols, nor make to yourselves molten gods: I am the Lord your God." And in other passages: "The children of Israel are my household servants; these are they whom I led forth from the land of Egypt: I am the Lord your God. Ye shall not make you idols fashioned by the hand, neither rear you up a graven image. Nor shall ye set up a remarkable stone in your land (to worship it): I am the Lord your God." These words indeed were first spoken by the Lord by the lips of Moses, being applicable certainly to whomsoever the Lord God of Israel may lead forth in like manner from the Egypt of a most superstitious world, and from the abode of human slavery. But from the mouth of every prophet in succession, sound forth also utterances of the same God, augmenting the same law of His by a renewal of the same commands, and in the first place announcing no other duty in so special a manner as the being on guard against all making and worshipping of idols; as when by the mouth of David He says: "The gods of the nations are silver and gold: they have eyes, and see not; they have ears, and hear not; they have a nose, and smell not; a mouth, and they speak not; hands, and they handle not; feet and they walk not. Like to them shall be they who make them, and trust in them."

Chapter III.

Nor should I think it needful to discuss whether God pursues a worthy course in forbidding His own name and honor to be given over to a lie, or does so in not consenting that such as He has plucked from the maze of false religion should return again to Egypt, or does so in not suffering to depart from Him them whom He has chosen for Himself. Thus that, too, will not require to be treated by us, whether He has wished to be kept the rule which He has chosen to appoint, and whether He justly avenges the abandonment of the rule which He has wished to be kept; since He would have appointed it to no purpose if He had not wished it kept, and would have to no purpose wished it kept if He had been unwilling to uphold it. My next step, indeed, is to put to the test these appointments of God in opposition to false religions, the completely vanquished as well as also the punished, since on these will depend the entire argument for martyrdoms. Moses was apart with God on the mountain, when the people, not brooking his absence, which was so needful, seek to make gods for themselves, which, for his own part, he will prefer to destroy. Aaron is importuned, and commands that the earrings of their women be brought together, that they may be thrown into the fire. For the people were about to lose, as a judgment upon themselves, the true ornaments for the ears, the words of God. The wise fire makes for them the molten likeness of a calf, reproaching them with having the heart where they have their treasure also, —in Egypt, to wit, which clothed with sacredness, among the other animals, a certain ox likewise. Therefore, the slaughter of three thousand by their nearest relatives, because they had displeased their so very near relative God, solemnly marked both the commencement and the deserts of the trespass. Israel having, as we are told in Numbers, turned aside at Sethim, the people go to the daughters of Moab to gratify their lust: they are allured to the idols, so that they committed whoredom with the spirit also: finally, they eat of their defiled sacrifices; then they both worship the gods of the nation, and are admitted to the rites of Beelphegor. For this lapse, too, into idolatry, sister to adultery, it took the slaughter of twenty-three thousand by the swords of their countrymen to appease the divine anger. After the death of Joshua the son of Nave they forsake the God of their fathers, and serve idols, Baalim and Ashtaroth; and the Lord in anger delivered them up to the hands of spoilers, and they continued to be spoiled by them, and to be sold to their adversaries, and could not at all stand before their enemies. Whithersoever they went forth, His hand was upon them for evil, and they were greatly distressed. And after this God sets judges (critas), the same as our censors, over them. But not even these did they continue steadfastly to obey. So soon as one of the judges died, they proceeded to transgress more than their fathers had done by going after the gods of others, and serving and worshipping them. Therefore, the Lord was angry. "Since, indeed," He says, "this nation has transgressed my covenant which I established with their fathers, and have not hearkened to my voice, I also will give no heed to remove from before them a man of the nations which Joshua left at his death." And thus, throughout almost all the annals of the judges and of the kings who succeeded them, while the strength of the surrounding nations was preserved, He meted wrath out to Israel by war and captivity and a foreign yoke, as often as they turned aside from Him, especially to idolatry.

Chapter IV.

If, therefore, it is evident that from the beginning this kind of worship has both been forbidden—witness the commands so numerous and weighty—and that it has never been engaged in without punishment following, as examples so numerous and impressive show, and that no offence is counted by God so presumptuous as a trespass of this sort, we ought further to perceive the purport of both the divine threatenings and their fulfilments, which was even then commended not only by the not calling in question, but also by the enduring of martyrdoms, for which certainly He had given occasion by forbidding idolatry. For otherwise martyrdoms would not take place. And certainly He had supplied, as a warrant for these, His own authority, willing those events to come to pass for the occurrence of which He had given occasion. At present (it is important), for we are getting severely stung concerning the will of God, and the scorpion repeats the prick, denying the existence of this will, finding fault with it, so that he either insinuates that there is another god, such that this is not his will, or none the less overthrows ours, seeing such is his will, or altogether denies this will of God, if he cannot deny Himself. But, for our part, contending elsewhere about God, and about all the rest of the body of heretical teaching, we now draw before us definite lines for one form of encounter, maintaining that this will, such as to have given occasion for martyrdoms, is that of not another god than the God of Israel, on the ground of the commandments relating to an always forbidden, as well as of the judgments upon a punished, idolatry. For if the keeping of a command involves the suffering of violence, this will be, so to speak, a command about keeping the command, requiring me to suffer that through which I shall be able to keep the command, violence namely, whatever of it threatens me when on my guard against idolatry. And certainly (in the case supposed) the Author of the command extorts compliance with it. He could not, therefore, have been unwilling that those events should come to pass by means of which the compliance will be manifest. The injunction is given me not to make mention of any other god, not even by speaking—as little by the tongue as by the hand—to fashion a god, and not to worship or in any way show reverence to another than Him only who thus commands me, whom I am both bid fear that I may not be forsaken by Him, and love with my whole being, that I may die for Him. Serving as a soldier under this oath, I am challenged by the enemy. If I surrender to them, I am as they are. In maintaining this oath, I fight furiously in battle, am wounded, hewn in pieces, slain. Who wished this fatal issue to his soldier, but he who sealed him by such an oath?

Chapter V.

You have therefore the will of my God. We have cured this prick. Let us give good heed to another thrust touching the character of His will. It would be tedious to show that my God is good—a truth with which the Marcionites have now been made acquainted by us. Meanwhile it is enough that He is called God for its being necessary that He should be believed to be good. For if anyone make the supposition that God is evil, he will not be able to take his stand on both the constituents thereof: he will be bound either to affirm that he whom he has thought to be evil is not God, or that he whom he has proclaimed to be God is good. Good, therefore, will be the will also of him who, unless he is good, will not be God. The goodness of the thing itself also which God has willed—of martyrdom, I mean—will show this, because only one who is good has willed what is good. I stoutly maintain that martyrdom is good, as required by the God by whom likewise idolatry is forbidden and punished. For martyrdom strives against and opposes idolatry. But to strive against and oppose evil cannot be ought but good. Not as if I denied that there is a rivalry in evil things with one another, as well as in good also; but this ground for it requires a different state of matters. For martyrdom contends with idolatry, not from some malice which they share, but from its own kindness; for it delivers from idolatry. Who will not proclaim that to be good which delivers from idolatry? What else is the opposition between idolatry and martyrdom, than that between life and death? Life will be counted to be martyrdom as much as idolatry to be death. He who will call life an evil, has death to speak of as a good. This frowardness also appertains to men—to discard what is wholesome, to accept what is baleful, to avoid all dangerous cures, or, in short, to be eager to die rather than to be healed. For they are many who flee from the aid of physic also, many in folly, many from fear and false modesty. And the healing art has manifestly an apparent cruelty, by reason of the lancet, and of the burning iron, and of the great heat of the mustard; yet to be cut and burned, and pulled and bitten, is not on that account an evil, for it occasions helpful pains; nor will it be refused merely because it afflicts, but because it afflicts inevitably will it be applied. The good accruing is the apology for the frightfulness of the work. In short, that man who is howling and groaning and bellowing in the hands of a physician will presently load the same hands with a fee, and proclaim that they are the best operators, and no longer affirm that they are cruel. Thus martyrdoms also rage furiously, but for salvation. God also will be at liberty to heal for everlasting life by means of fires and swords, and all that is painful. But you will admire the physician at least even in that respect, that for the most part he employs like properties in the cures to counteract the properties of the diseases, when he aids, as it were, the wrong way, succoring by means of those things to which the affliction is owing. For he both checks heat by heat, by laying on a greater load; and subdues inflammation by leaving thirst unappeased, by tormenting rather; and contracts the superabundance of bile by every bitter little draught, and stops hemorrhage by opening a veinlet in addition. But you will think that God must be found fault with, and that for being jealous, if He has chosen to contend with a disease and to do good by imitating the malady, to destroy death by death, to dissipate killing by killing, to dispel tortures by tortures, to disperse punishments by punishments, to bestow life by withdrawing it, to aid the flesh by injuring it, to preserve the soul by snatching it away. The wrongheadedness, as you deem it to be, is reasonableness; what you count cruelty is kindness.

Thus, seeing God by brief (sufferings) effects cures for eternity, extol your God for your prosperity; you have fallen into His hands, but have happily fallen. He also fell into your sicknesses. Man always first provides employment for the physician; in short, he has brought upon himself the danger of death. He had received from his own Lord, as from a physician, the salutary enough rule to live according to the law, that he should eat of all indeed (that the garden produced) and should refrain from only one little tree which in the meantime the Physician Himself knew as a perilous one. He gave ear to him whom he preferred, and broke through self-restraint. He ate what was forbidden, and, surfeited by the trespass, suffered indigestion tending to death; he certainly richly deserving to lose his life altogether who wished to do so. But the inflamed tumor due to the trespass having been endured until in due time the medicine might be mixed, the Lord gradually prepared the means of healing—all the rules of faith, they also bearing a resemblance to (the causes of) the ailment, seeing they annul the word of death by the word of life, and diminish the trespass-listening by a listening of allegiance. Thus, even when that Physician commands one to die, He drives out the lethargy of death. Why does man show reluctance to suffer now from a cure, what he was not reluctant then to suffer from a disorder? Does he dislike being killed for salvation, who did not dislike being killed for destruction? —Will he feel squeamish with reference to the counter poison, who gaped for the poison?

Chapter VI.

But if, for the contest's sake, God had appointed martyrdoms for us, that thereby we might make trial with our opponent, in order that He may now keep bruising him by whom man chose to be bruised, here too generosity rather than harshness in God holds sway. For He wished to make man, now plucked from the devil's throat by faith, trample upon him likewise by courage, that he might not merely have escaped from, but also completely vanquished, his enemy. He who had called to salvation has been pleased to summon to glory also, that they who were rejoicing in consequence of their deliverance may be in transports when they are crowned likewise. With what good-will the world celebrates those games, the combative festivals and superstitious contests of the Greeks, involving forms both of worship and of pleasure, has now become clear in Africa also. As yet cities, by sending their congratulations severally, annoy Carthage, which was presented with the Pythian game after the racecourse had attained to an old age. Thus, by the world it has been believed to be a most proper mode of testing proficiency in studies, to put in competition the forms of skill, to elicit the existing condition of bodies and of voices, the reward being the informer, the public exhibition the judge, and pleasure the decision. Where there are mere contests, there are some wounds: fists make reel, heels kick like butting rams, boxing-gloves mangle, whips leave gashes. Yet there will be no one reproaching the superintendent of the contest for exposing men to outrage. Suits for injuries lie outside the racecourse. But to the extent that those persons deal in discoloration, and gore, and swellings, he will design for them crowns, doubtless, and glory, and a present, political privileges, contributions by the citizens, images, statues, and—of such sort as the world can give—an eternity of fame, a resurrection by being kept in remembrance. The pugilist himself does not complain of feeling pain, for he wishes it; the crown closes the wounds, the palm hides the blood: he is excited more by victory than by injury. Will you count this man hurt whom you see happy? But not even the vanquished himself will reproach the superintendent of the contest for his misfortune. Shall it be unbecoming in God to bring forth kinds of skill and rules of His own into public view, into this open ground of the world, to be seen by men, and angels, and all powers?—to test flesh and spirit as to steadfastness and endurance?—to give to this one the palm, to this one distinction, to that one the privilege of citizenship, to that one pay?—to reject some also, and after punishing to remove them with disgrace? You dictate to God, forsooth, the times, or the ways, or the places in which to institute a trial concerning His own troop (of competitors) as if it were not proper for the Judge to pronounce the preliminary decision also. Well now, if He had put forth faith to suffer martyrdoms not for the contest's sake, but for its own benefit, ought it not to have had some store of hope, for the increase of which it might restrain desire of its own, and check its wish in order that it might strive to mount up, seeing they also who discharge earthly functions are eager for promotion? Or how will there be many mansions in our Father's house, if not to accord with a diversity of deserts? How will one star also differ from another star in glory, unless in virtue of disparity in their rays? But further, if, on that account, some increase of brightness also was appropriate to loftiness of faith, that gain ought to have been of some such sort as would cost great effort, poignant suffering, torture, death. But consider the requital, when flesh and life are paid away—than which in man there is naught more precious, the one from the hand of God, the other from His breath—that the very things are paid away in obtaining the benefit of which the benefit consists; that the very things are expended which may be acquired; that the same things are the price which are also the commodities. God had foreseen also other weaknesses incident to the condition of man—the stratagems of the enemy, the deceptive aspects of the creatures, the snares of the world; that faith, even after baptism, would be endangered; that the most, after attaining unto salvation, would be lost again, through soiling the wedding-dress, through failing to provide oil for their torchlets—would be such as would have to be sought for over mountains and woodlands, and carried back upon the shoulders. He therefore appointed as second supplies of comfort, and the last means of succor, the fight of martyrdom and the baptism—thereafter free from danger—of blood. And concerning the happiness of the man who has partaken of these, David says: "Blessed are they whose iniquities are forgiven, and whose sins are covered. Blessed is the man to whom the Lord will not impute sin." For, strictly speaking, there cannot any longer be reckoned ought against the martyrs, by whom in the baptism (of blood) life itself is laid down. Thus, "love covers the multitude of sins;" and loving God, to wit, with all its strength (by which in the endurance of martyrdom it maintains the fight), with all its life (which it lays down for God), it makes of man a martyr. Shall you call these cures, counsels, methods of judging, spectacles, (illustrations of) even the barbarity of God? Does God covet man's blood? And yet I might venture to affirm that He does, if man also covets the kingdom of heaven, if man covets a sure salvation, if man also covets a second new birth. The exchange is displeasing to no one, which can plead, in justification of itself, that either benefit or injury is shared by the parties making it.

Chapter VII.

If the scorpion, swinging his tail in the air, still reproach us with having a murderer for our God, I shall shudder at the altogether foul breath of blasphemy which comes stinking from his heretical mouth; but I will embrace even such a God, with assurance derived from reason, by which reason even He Himself has, in the person of His own Wisdom, by the lips of Solomon, proclaimed Himself to be more than a murderer: Wisdom (Sophia), says He has slain her own children. Sophiais Wisdom. She has certainly slain them wisely if only into life, and reasonably if only into glory. Of murder by a parent, oh the clever form! Oh the dexterity of crime! Oh the proof of cruelty, which has slain for this reason, that he whom it may have slain may not die! And therefore what follows? Wisdom is praised in hymns, in the places of egress; for the death of martyrs also is praised in song. Wisdom behaves with firmness in the streets, for with good results does she murder her own sons. Nay, on the top of the walls she speaks with assurance, when indeed, according to Esaias, this one calls out, "I am God's;" and this one shouts, "In the name of Jacob;" and another writes, "In the name of Israel." O good mother! I myself also wish to be put among the number of her sons, that I may be slain by her; I wish to be slain, that I may become a son. But does she merely murder her sons, or also torture them? For I hear God also, in another passage, say, "I will burn them as gold is burned, and will try them as silver is tried." Certainly by the means of torture which fires and punishments supply, by the testing martyrdoms of faith. The apostle also knows what kind of God he has ascribed to us, when he writes: "If God spared not His own Son, but gave Him up for us, how did He not with Him also give us all things?" You see how divine Wisdom has murdered even her own proper, first-born and only Son, who is certainly about to live, nay, to bring back the others also into life. I can say with the Wisdom of God; It is Christ who gave Himself up for our offences. Already has Wisdom butchered herself also. The character of words depends not on the sound only, but on the meaning also, and they must be heard not merely by ears, but also by minds. He who does not understand, believes God to be cruel; although for him also who does not understand, an announcement has been made to restrain his harshness in understanding otherwise than aright. "For who," says the apostle, "has known the mind of the Lord? or who has been His counsellor, to teach Him? or who has pointed out to Him the way of understanding?" But, indeed, the world has held it lawful for Diana of the Scythians, or Mercury of the Gauls, or Saturn of the Africans, to be appeased by human sacrifices; and in Latium to this day Jupiter has human blood given him to taste in the midst of the city; and no one makes it a matter of discussion, or imagines that it does not occur for some reason, or that it occurs by the will of his God, without having value. If our God, too, to have a sacrifice of His own, had required martyrdoms for Himself, who would have reproached Him for the deadly religion, and the mournful ceremonies, and the altar-pyre, and the undertaker-priest, and not rather have counted happy the man whom God should have devoured?

Chapter VIII.

We keep therefore the one position, and, in respect of this question only, summon to an encounter, whether martyrdoms have been commanded by God, that you may believe that they have been commanded by reason, if you know that they have been commanded by Him, because God will not command ought without reason. Since the death of His own saints is precious is His sight, as David sings, it is not, I think, that one which falls to the lot of men generally, and is a debt due by all (rather is that one even disgraceful on account of the trespass, and the desert of condemnation to which it is to be traced), but that other which is met in this very work—in bearing witness for religion, and maintaining the fight of confession in behalf of righteousness and the sacrament. As saith Esaias, "See how the righteous man perisheth, and no one layeth it to heart; and righteous men are taken away, and no one considereth it: for from before the face of unrighteousness the righteous man perisheth, and he shall have honor at his burial." Here, too, you have both an announcement of martyrdoms, and of the recompense they bring. From the beginning, indeed, righteousness suffers violence. Forthwith, as soon as God has begun to be worshipped, religion has got ill-will for her portion. He who had pleased God is slain, and that by his brother. Beginning with kindred blood, in order that it might the more easily go in quest of that of strangers, ungodliness made the object of its pursuit, finally, that not only of righteous persons, but even of prophets also. David is persecuted; Elias put to flight; Jeremias stoned; Esaias cut asunder; Zacharias butchered between the altar and the temple, imparting to the hard stones lasting marks of his blood. That person himself, at the close of the law and the prophets, and called not a prophet, but a messenger, is, suffering an ignominious death, beheaded to reward a dancing-girl. And certainly they who were wont to be led by the Spirit of God used to be guided by Himself to martyrdoms; so that they had even already to endure what they had also proclaimed as requiring to be borne. Wherefore the brotherhood of the three also, when the dedication of the royal image was the occasion of the citizens being pressed to offer worship, knew well what faith, which alone in them had not been taken captive, required—namely, that they must resist idolatry to the death. For they remembered also the words of Jeremias writing to those over whom that captivity was impending: "And now ye shall see borne upon (men's) shoulders the gods of the Babylonians, of gold and silver and wood, causing fear to the Gentiles. Beware, therefore, that ye also do not be altogether like the foreigners, and be seized with fear while ye behold crowds worshipping those gods before and behind, but say in your mind, Our duty is to worship Thee, O Lord." Therefore, having got confidence from God, they said, when with strength of mind they set at defiance the king's threats against the disobedient: "There is no necessity for our making answer to this command of yours. For our God whom we worship is able to deliver us from the furnace of fire and from your hands; and then it will be made plain to you that we shall neither serve your idol, nor worship your golden image which you have set up." O martyrdom even without suffering perfect! Enough did they suffer! enough were they burned, whom on this account God shielded, that it might not seem that they had given a false representation of His power. For forthwith, certainly, would the lions, with their pent-up and wonted savageness, have devoured Daniel also, a worshipper of none but God, and therefore accused and demanded by the Chaldeans, if it had been right that the worthy anticipation of Darius concerning God should have proved delusive. For the rest, every preacher of God, and every worshipper also, such as, having been summoned to the service of idolatry, had refused compliance, ought to have suffered, agreeably to the tenor of that argument too, by which the truth ought to have been recommended both to those who were then living and to those following in succession—(namely), that the suffering of its defenders themselves bespeak trust for it, because nobody would have been willing to be slain but one possessing the truth. Such commands as well as instances, remounting to earliest times, show that believers are under obligation to suffer martyrdom.

Chapter IX.

It remains for us, lest ancient times may perhaps have had the sacrament (exclusively) their own, to review the modern Christian system, as though, being also from God, it might be different from what preceded, and besides, therefore, opposed thereto in its code of rules likewise, so that its Wisdom knows not to murder her own sons! Evidently, in the case of Christ both the divine nature and the will and the sect are different from any previously known! He will have commanded either no martyrdoms at all, or those which must be understood in a sense different from the ordinary, being such a person as to urge no one to a risk of this kind as to promise no reward to them who suffer for Him, because He does not wish them to suffer; and therefore does He say, when setting forth His chief commands, "Blessed are they who are persecuted for righteousness' sake, for theirs is the kingdom of heaven." The following statement, indeed, applies first to all without restriction, then specially to the apostles themselves: "Blessed shall ye be when men shall revile you, and persecute you, and shall say all manner of evil against you, for my sake. Rejoice and be exceeding glad, since very great is your reward in heaven; for so used their fathers to do even to the prophets." So that He likewise foretold their having to be themselves also slain, after the example of the prophets. Though, even if He had appointed all this persecution in case He were obeyed for those only who were then apostles, assuredly through them along with the entire sacrament, with the shoot of the name, with the layer of the Holy Spirit, the rule about enduring persecution also would have had respect to us too, as to disciples by inheritance, and, (as it were,) bushes from the apostolic seed. For even thus again does He address words of guidance to the apostles: "Behold, I send you forth as sheep in the midst of wolves;" and, "Beware of men, for they will deliver you up to the councils, and they will scourge you in their synagogues; and ye shall be brought before governors and kings for my sake, for a testimony against them and the Gentiles," etc. Now when He adds, "But the brother will deliver up the brother to death, and the father the child; and the children shall rise up against their parents, and cause them to be put to death," He has clearly announced with reference to the others, (that they would be subjected to) this form of unrighteous conduct, which we do not find exemplified in the case of the apostles. For none of them had experience of a father or a brother as a betrayer, which very many of us have. Then He returns to the apostles: "And ye shall be hated of all men for my name's sake." How much more shall we, for whom there exists the necessity of being delivered up by parents too! Thus, by allotting this very betrayal, now to the apostles, now to all, He pours out the same destruction upon all the possessors of the name, on whom the name, along with the condition that it be an object of hatred, will rest. But he who will endure on to the end—this man will be saved. By enduring what but persecution,—betrayal,—death? For to endure to the end is naught else than to suffer the end. And therefore there immediately follow, "The disciple is not above his master, nor the servant above his own lord;" because, seeing the Master and Lord Himself was steadfast in suffering persecution, betrayal and death, much more will it be the duty of His servants and disciples to bear the same, that they may not seem as if superior to Him, or to have got an immunity from the assaults of unrighteousness, since this itself should be glory enough for them, to be conformed to the sufferings of their Lord and Master; and, preparing them for the endurance of these, He reminds them that they must not fear such persons as kill the body only, but are not able to destroy the soul, but that they must dedicate fear to Him rather who has such power that He can kill both body and soul, and destroy them in hell. Who, pray, are these slayers of the body only, but the governors and kings aforesaid—men, I ween? Who is the ruler of the soul also, but God only? Who is this but the threatener of fires hereafter, He without whose will not even one of two sparrows falls to the ground; that is, not even one of the two substances of man, flesh or spirit, because the number of our hairs also has been recorded before Him? Fear ye not, therefore. When He adds, "Ye are of more value than many sparrows," He makes promise that we shall not in vain—that is, not without profit—fall to the ground if we choose to be killed by men rather than by God. "Whosoever therefore will confess in me before men, in him will I confess also before my Father who is in heaven; and whosoever shall deny me before men, him will I deny also before my Father who is in heaven." Clear, as I think, are the terms used in announcing, and the way to explain, the confession as well as the denial, although the mode of putting them is different. He who confesses himself a Christian, beareth witness that he is Christ's; he who is Christ's must be in Christ. If he is in Christ, he certainly confesses in Christ, when he confesses himself a Christian. For he cannot be this without being in Christ. Besides, by confessing in Christ he confesses Christ too: since, by virtue of being a Christian, he is in Christ, while Christ Himself also is in him. For if you have made mention of day, you have also held out to view the element of light which gives us day, although you may not have made mention of light. Thus, albeit He has not expressly said, "He who will confess me," (yet) the conduct involved in daily confession is not different from what is meant in our Lord's declaration. For he who confesses himself to be what he is, that is, a Christian, confesses that likewise by which he is it, that is, Christ. Therefore, he who has denied that he is a Christian, has denied in Christ, by denying that he is in Christ while he denies that he is a Christian; and, on the other hand, by denying that Christ is in him, while He denies that he is in Christ, he will deny Christ too. Thus both he who will deny in Christ, will deny Christ, and he who will confess in Christ will confess Christ. It would have been enough, therefore, though our Lord had made an announcement about confessing merely. For, from His mode of presenting confession, it might be decided beforehand with reference to its opposite too—denial, that is—that denial is repaid by the Lord with denial, just as confession is with confession. And therefore, since in the mold in which the confession has been cast the state of (the case with reference to) denial also may be perceived, it is evident that to another manner of denial belongs what the Lord has announced concerning it, in terms different from those in which He speaks of confession, when He says, "Who will deny me," not "Who will deny in me." For He had foreseen that this form of violence also would, for the most part, immediately follow when any one had been forced to renounce the Christian name—that he who had denied that he was a Christian would be compelled to deny Christ Himself too by blaspheming Him. As not long ago, alas, we shuddered at the struggle waged in this way by some with their entire faith, which had had favorable omens. Therefore, it will be to no purpose to say, "Though I shall deny that I am a Christian, I shall not be denied by Christ, for I have not denied Himself." For even so much will be inferred from that denial, by which, seeing he denies Christ in him by denying that he is a Christian, he has denied Christ Himself also. But there is more, because He threatens likewise shame with shame (in return): "Whosoever shall be ashamed of me before men, of him will I also be ashamed before my Father who is in heaven." For He was aware that denial is produced even most of all by shame, that the state of the mind appears in the forehead, and that the wound of shame precedes that in the body.

Chapter X.

But as to those who think that not here, that is, not within this environment of earth, nor during this period of existence, nor before men possessing this nature shared by us all, has confession been appointed to be made, what a supposition is theirs, being at variance with the whole order of things of which we have experience in these lands, and in this life, and under human authorities! Doubtless, when the souls have departed from their bodies, and begun to be put upon trial in the several stories of the heavens, with reference to the engagement (under which they have come to Jesus), and to be questioned about those hidden mysteries of the heretics, they must then confess before the real powers and the real men—the Teleti, to wit, and the Abascanti, and the Acineti of Valentinus! For, say they, even the Demiurge himself did not uniformly approve of the men of our world, whom he counted as a drop of a bucket, and the dust of the threshing-floor, and spittle and locusts, and put on a level even with brute beasts. Clearly, it is so written. Yet not therefore must we understand that there is, besides us, another kind of man, which—for it is evidently thus (in the case proposed)—has been able to assume without invalidating a comparison between the two kinds, both the characteristics of the race and a unique property. For even if the life was tainted, so that condemned to contempt it might be likened to objects held in contempt, the nature was not forthwith taken away, so that there might be supposed to be another under its name. Rather is the nature preserved, though the life blushes; nor does Christ know other men than those with reference to whom He says, "Whom do men say that I am?" And, "As ye would that men should do to you, do ye likewise so to, them." Consider whether He may not have preserved a race such that He is looking for a testimony to Himself from them, as well as consisting of those on whom He enjoins the interchange of righteous dealing. But if I should urgently demand that those heavenly men be described to me,

Aratus will sketch more easily Perseus and Cepheus, and Erigone, and Ariadne, among the constellations. But who prevented the Lord from clearly prescribing that confession by men likewise has to be made where He plainly announced that His own would be; so that the statement might have run thus:" Whosoever shall confess in me before men in heaven, I also will confess in him before my Father who is in heaven?" He ought to have saved me from this mistake about confession on earth, which He would not have wished me to take part in, if He had commanded one in heaven; for I knew no other men but the inhabitants of the earth, man himself even not having up to that time been observed in heaven. Besides, what is the credibility of the things (alleged), that, being after death raised to heavenly places, I should be put to the test there, whither I would not be translated without being already tested, that I should there be tried in reference to a command where I could not come, but to find admittance? Heaven lies open to the Christian before the way to it does; because there is no way to heaven, but to him to whom heaven lies open; and he who reaches it will enter. What powers, keeping guard at the gate, do I hear you affirm to exist in accordance with Roman superstition, with a certain Carnus, Forculus, and Limentinus? What powers do you set in order at the railings? If you have ever read in David, "Lift up your gates, ye princes, and let the everlasting gates be lifted up; and the King of glory shall enter in;" if you have also heard from Amos, "Who buildeth up to the heavens his way of ascent, and is such as to pour forth his abundance (of waters) over the earth;" know that both that way of ascent was thereafter levelled with the ground, by the footsteps of the Lord, and an entrance thereafter opened up by the might of Christ, and that no delay or inquest will meet Christians on the threshold, since they have there to be not discriminated from one another, but owned, and not put to the question, but received in. For though you think heaven still shut, remember that the Lord left here to Peter and through him to the Church, the keys of it, which everyone who has been here put to the question, and also made confession, will carry with him. But the devil stoutly affirms that we must confess there, to persuade us that we must deny here. I shall send before me fine documents, to be sure, I shall carry with me excellent keys, the fear of them who kill the body only, but do naught against the soul: I shall be graced by the neglect of this command: I shall stand with credit in heavenly places, who could not stand in earthly: I shall hold out against the greater powers, who yielded to the lesser: I shall deserve to be at length let in, though now shut out. It readily occurs to one to remark further, "If it is in heaven that men must confess, it is here too that they must deny." For where the one is, there both are. For contraries always go together. There will need to be carried on in heaven persecution even, which is the occasion of confession or denial. Why, then, do you refrain, O most presumptuous heretic, from transporting to the world above the whole series of means proper to the intimidation of Christians, and especially to put there the very hatred for the name, where Christ rules at the right hand of the Father? Will you plant there both synagogues of the Jews—fountains of persecution—before which the apostles endured the scourge, and heathen assemblages with their own circus, forsooth, where they readily join in the cry, Death to the third race? But ye are bound to produce in the same place both our brothers, fathers, children, mothers in-law, daughters-in-law and those of our household, through whose agency the betrayal has been appointed; likewise, kings, governors, and armed authorities, before whom the matter at issue must be contested. Assuredly there will be in heaven a prison also, destitute of the sun's rays or full of light unthankfully, and fetters of the zones perhaps, and, for a rack-horse, the axis itself which whirls the heavens around. Then, if a Christian is to be stoned, hail-storms will be near; if burned, thunderbolts are at hand; if butchered, the armed Orion will exercise his function; if put an end to by beasts, the north will send forth the bears, the Zodiac the bulls and the lions. He who will endure these assaults to the end, the same shall be saved.

Will there be then, in heaven, both an end, and suffering, a killing, and the first confession? And where will be the flesh requisite for all this? Where the body which alone has to be killed by men? Unerring reason has commanded us to set forth these things in even a playful manner; nor will anyone thrust out the bar consisting in this objection (we have offered), so as not to be compelled to transfer the whole array of means proper to persecution, all the powerful instrumentality which has been provided for dealing with this matter, to the place where he has put the court before which confession should be made. Since confession is elicited by persecution, and persecution ended in confession, there cannot but be at the same time, in attendance upon these, the instrumentality which determines both the entrance and the exit, that is, the beginning and the end. But both hatred for the name will be here, persecution breaks out here, betrayal brings men forth here, examination uses force here, torture rages here, and confession or denial completes this whole course of procedure on the earth. Therefore, if the other things are here, confession also is not elsewhere; if confession is elsewhere, the other things also are not here. Certainly the other things are not elsewhere; therefore, neither is confession in heaven. Or, if they will have it that the manner in which the heavenly examination and confession take place is different, it will certainly be also incumbent on them to devise a mode of procedure of their own of a very different kind, and opposed to that method which is indicated in the Scriptures. And we may be able to say, let them consider (whether what they imagine to exist does so), if so be that this course of procedure, proper to examination and confession on earth—a course which has persecution as the source in which it originates, and which pleads dissension in the state—is preserved to its own faith, if so be that we must believe just as is also written, and understand just as is spoken. Here I endure the entire course (in question), the Lord Himself not appointing a different quarter of the world for my doing so. For what does He add after finishing with confession and denial? "Think not that I am come to send peace on earth, but a sword,"—undoubtedly on the earth. "For I am come to set a man at variance against his father, and the daughter against her mother, and the mother-in-law against her daughter-in-law. And a man's foes shall be they of his own household." For so is it brought to pass, that the brother delivers up the brother to death, and the father the son: and the children rise up against the parents, and cause them to die. And he who endureth to the end let that man be saved. So that this whole course of procedure characteristic of the Lord's sword, which has been sent not to heaven, but to earth, makes confession also to be there, which by enduring to the end is to issue in the suffering of death.

Chapter XI.

In the same manner, therefore, we maintain that the other announcements too refer to the condition of martyrdom. "He," says Jesus, "who will value his own life also more than me, is not worthy of me,"—that is, he who will rather live by denying, than die by confessing, me; and "he who findeth his life shall lose it; but he who loseth it for my sake shall find it." Therefore, indeed he finds it, who, in winning life, denies; but he who thinks that he wins it by denying, will lose it in hell. On the other hand, he who, through confessing, is killed, will lose it for the present, but is also about to find it unto everlasting life. In fine, governors themselves, when they urge men to deny, say, "Save your life;" and, "Do not lose your life." How would Christ speak, but in accordance with the treatment to which the Christian would be subjected? But when He forbids thinking about what answer to make at a judgment-seat, He is preparing His own servants for what awaited them, He gives the assurance that the Holy Spirit will answer by them; and when He wishes a brother to be visited in prison, He is commanding that those about to confess be the object of solicitude; and He is soothing their sufferings when He asserts that God will avenge His own elect. In the parable also of the withering of the word after the green blade had sprung up, He is drawing a picture with reference to the burning heat of persecutions. If these announcements are not understood as they are made, without doubt they signify something else than the sound indicates; and there will be one thing in the words, another in their meanings, as is the case with allegories, with parables, with riddles. Whatever wind of reasoning, therefore, these scorpions may catch (in their sails), with whatever subtlety they may attack, there is now one line of defense: an appeal will be made to the facts themselves, whether they occur as the Scriptures represent that they would; since another thing will then be meant in the Scriptures if that very one (which seems to be so) is not found in actual facts. For what is written, must needs come to pass. Besides, what is written will then come to pass, if something different does not. But, lo! we are both regarded as persons to be hated by all men for the sake of the name, as it is written; and are delivered up by our nearest of kin also, as it is written; and are brought before magistrates, and examined, and tortured, and make confession, and are ruthlessly killed, as it is written. So the Lord ordained. If He ordained these events otherwise, why do they not come to pass otherwise than He ordained them, that is, as He ordained them? And yet they do not come to pass otherwise than He ordained. Therefore, as they come to pass, so He ordained; and as He ordained, so they come to pass. For neither would they have been permitted to occur otherwise than He ordained, nor for His part would He have ordained otherwise than He would wish them to occur. Thus these passages of Scripture will not mean ought else than we recognize in actual facts; or if those events are not yet taking place which are announced, how are those taking place which have not been announced? For these events which are taking place have not been announced, if those which are announced are different, and not these which are taking place. Well now, seeing the very occurrences are met with in actual life which are believed to have been expressed with a different meaning in words, what would happen if they were found to have come to pass in a different manner than had been revealed? But this will be the waywardness of faith, not to believe what has been demonstrated, to assume the truth of what has not been demonstrated. And to this waywardness I will offer the following objection also, that if these events, which occur as is written, will not be the very ones which are announced, those too (which are meant) ought not to occur as is written, that they themselves also may not, after the example of these others, be in danger of exclusion, since there is one thing in the words and another in the facts; and there remains that even the events which have been announced are not seen when they occur, if they are announced otherwise than they have to occur. And how will those be believed (to have come to pass), which will not have been announced as they come to pass? Thus heretics, by not believing what is announced as it has been shown to have taken place, believe what has not been even announced.

Chapter XII.

Who, now, should know better the marrow of the Scriptures than the school of Christ itself?—the persons whom the Lord both chose for Himself as scholars, certainly to be fully instructed in all points, and appointed to us for masters to instruct us in all points. To whom would He have rather made known the veiled import of His own language, than to him to whom He disclosed the likeness of His own glory—to Peter, John, and James, and afterwards to Paul, to whom He granted participation in (the joys of) paradise too, prior to his martyrdom? Or do they also write differently from what they think—teachers using deceit, not truth? Addressing the Christians of Pontus, Peter, at all events, says, "How great indeed is the glory, if ye suffer patiently, without being punished as evildoers! For this is a lovely feature, and even hereunto were ye called, since Christ also suffered for us, leaving you Himself as an example, that ye should follow His own steps." And again: "Beloved, be not alarmed by the fiery trial which is taking place among you, as though some strange thing happened unto you. For, inasmuch as ye are partakers of Christ's sufferings, do ye rejoice; that, when His glory shall be revealed, ye may be glad also with exceeding joy. If ye are reproached for the name of Christ, happy are ye; because glory and the Spirit of God rest upon you: if only none of you suffer as a murderer, or as a thief, or as an evil-doer, or as a busybody in other men's matters; yet (if any man suffer) as a Christian, let him not be ashamed, but let him glorify God on this behalf." John, in fact, exhorts us to lay down our lives even for our brethren, affirming that there is no fear in love: "For perfect love casteth out fear, since fear has punishment; and he who fears is not perfect in love." What fear would it be better to understand (as here meant), than that which gives rise to denial? What love does he assert to be perfect, but that which puts fear to flight, and gives courage to confess? What penalty will he appoint as the punishment of fear, but that which he who denies is about to pay, who has to be slain, body and soul, in hell? And if he teaches that we must die for the brethren, how much more for the Lord—he being sufficiently prepared, by his own Revelation too, for giving such advice! For indeed the Spirit had sent the injunction to the angel of the church in Smyrna: "Behold, the devil shall cast some of you into prison, that ye may be tried ten days. Be thou faithful unto death, and I will give thee a crown of life." Also to the angel of the church in Pergamus (mention was made) of Antipas, the very faithful martyr, who was slain where Satan dwelleth. Also to the angel of the church in Philadelphia (it was signified) that he who had not denied the name of the Lord was delivered from the last trial. Then to every conqueror the Spirit promises now the tree of life, and exemption from the second death; now the hidden manna with the stone of glistening whiteness, and the name unknown (to every man save him that receiveth it); now power to rule with a rod of iron, and the brightness of the morning star; now the being clothed in white raiment, and not having the name blotted out of the book of life, and being made in the temple of God a pillar with the inscription on it of the name of God and of the Lord, and of the heavenly Jerusalem; now a sitting with the Lord on His throne,—which once was persistently refused to the sons of Zebedee. Who, pray, are these so blessed conquerors, but martyrs in the strict sense of the word? For indeed theirs are the victories whose also are the fights; theirs, however, are the fights whose also is the blood. But the souls of the martyrs both peacefully rest in the meantime under the altar, and support their patience by the assured hope of revenge; and, clothed in their robes, wear the dazzling halo of brightness, until others also may fully share in their glory. For yet again a countless throng are revealed, clothed in white and distinguished by palms of victory, celebrating their triumph doubtless over Antichrist, since one of the elders says, "These are they who come out of that great tribulation, and have washed their robes, and made them white in the blood of the Lamb." For the flesh is the clothing of the soul. The uncleanness, indeed, is washed away by baptism, but the stains are changed into dazzling whiteness by martyrdom. For Esaias also promises, that out of red and scarlet there will come forth the whiteness of snow and wool. When great Babylon likewise is represented as drunk with the blood of the saints, doubtless the supplies needful for her drunkenness are furnished by the cups of martyrdoms; and what suffering the fear of martyrdoms will entail, is in like manner shown. For among all the castaways, nay, taking precedence of them all, are the fearful. "But the fearful," says John—and then come the others— "will have their part in the lake of fire and brimstone." Thus fear, which, as stated in his epistle, love drives out, has punishment.

Chapter XIII.

But how Paul, an apostle, from being a persecutor, who first of all shed the blood of the church, though afterwards he exchanged the sword for the pen, and turned the dagger into a plough, being first a ravening wolf of Benjamin, then himself supplying food as did Jacob—how he, (I say,) speaks in favor of martyrdoms, now to be chosen by himself also, when, rejoicing over the Thessalonians, he says, "So that we glory in you in the churches of God, for your patience and faith in all your persecutions and tribulations, in which ye endure a manifestation of the righteous judgment of God, that ye may be accounted worthy of His kingdom, for which ye also suffer!" As also in his Epistle to the Romans: "And not only so, but we glory in tribulations also, being sure that tribulation worketh patience, and patience experience, and experience hope; and hope maketh not ashamed." And again: "And if children, then heirs, heirs indeed of God, and joint-heirs with Christ: if so be that we suffer with Him, that we may be also glorified together. For I reckon that the sufferings of this time are not worthy to be compared with the glory which shall be revealed in us." And therefore, he afterward says: "Who shall separate us from the love of God? Shall tribulation, or distress, or famine, or nakedness, or peril, or sword? (As it is written: For Thy sake we are killed all the day long; we have been counted as sheep for the slaughter.) Nay, in all these things we are more than conquerors, through Him who loved us. For we are persuaded, that neither death, nor life, nor power, nor height, nor depth, nor any other creature, shall be able to separate us from the love of God, which is in Christ Jesus our Lord." But further, in recounting his own sufferings to the Corinthians, he certainly decided that suffering must be borne: "In labors, (he says,) more abundant, in prisons very frequent, in deaths oft. Of the Jews five times received I forty stripes, save one; thrice was I beaten with rods; once was I stoned," and the rest. And if these severities will seem to be more grievous than martyrdoms, yet once more he says: "Therefore I take pleasure in infirmities, in reproaches, in necessities, in persecutions, in distresses for Christ's sake." He also says, in verses occurring in a previous part of the epistle: "Our condition is such, that we are troubled on every side, yet not distressed; and are in need, but not in utter want; since we are harassed by persecutions, but not forsaken; it is such that we are cast down, but not destroyed; always bearing about in our body the dying of Christ." "But though," says he, "our outward man perisheth"—the flesh doubtless, by the violence of persecutions— "yet the inward man is renewed day by day"—the soul, doubtless, by hope in the promises. "For our light affliction, which is but for a moment, worketh for us a far more exceeding and eternal weight of glory; while we look not at the things which are seen, but at the things which are not seen. For the things which are seen are temporal"—he is speaking of troubles; "but the things which are not seen are eternal"—he is promising rewards. But writing in bonds to the Thessalonians, he certainly affirmed that they were blessed, since to them it had been given not only to believe on Christ, but also to suffer for His sake. "Having," says he, "the same conflict which ye both saw in me, and now hear to be in me." "For though I am offered upon the sacrifice, I joy and rejoice with you all; in like manner do ye also joy and rejoice with me." You see what he decides the bliss of martyrdom to be, in honor of which he is providing a festival of mutual joy. When at length he had come to be very near the attainment of his desire, greatly rejoicing in what he saw before him, he writes in these terms to Timothy: "For I am already being offered, and the time of my departure is at hand. I have fought the good fight, I have finished my course, I have kept the faith; there is laid up for me the crown which the Lord will give me on that day"—doubtless of his suffering. Admonition enough did he for his part also give in preceding passages: "It is a faithful saying: For if we are dead with Christ, we shall also live with Him; if we suffer, we shall also reign with Him; if we deny Him, He also will deny us; if we believe not, yet He is faithful: He cannot deny Himself." "Be not thou, therefore, ashamed of the testimony of our Lord, nor of me His prisoner;" for he had said before: "For God hath not given us the spirit of fear, but of power, and of love, and of a sound mind." For we suffer with power from love toward God, and with a sound mind, when we suffer for our blamelessness. But further, if He anywhere enjoins endurance, for what more than for sufferings is He providing it? If anywhere He tears men away from idolatry, what more than martyrdoms takes the lead, in tearing them away to its injury?

Chapter XIV.

No doubt the apostle admonishes the Romans to be subject to all power, because there is no power but of God, and because (the ruler) does not carry the sword without reason, and is the servant of God, nay also, says he, a revenger to execute wrath upon him that doeth evil. For he had also previously spoken thus: "For rulers are not a terror to a good work, but to an evil. Wilt thou then not be afraid of the power? Do that which is good, and thou shalt have praise of it. Therefore, he is a minister of God to thee for good. But if thou do that which is evil, be afraid." Thus he bids you be subject to the powers, not on an opportunity occurring for his avoiding martyrdom, but when he is making an appeal in behalf of a good life, under the view also of their being as it were assistants bestowed upon righteousness, as it were handmaids of the divine court of justice, which even here pronounces sentence beforehand upon the guilty. Then he goes on also to show how he wishes you to be subject to the powers, bidding you pay "tribute to whom tribute is due, custom to whom custom," that is, the things which are Cæsar's to Cæsar, and the things which are God's to God; but man is the property of God alone. Peter, no doubt, had likewise said that the king indeed must be honored, yet so that the king be honored only when he keeps to his own sphere, when he is far from assuming divine honors; because both father and mother will be loved along with God, not put on an equality with Him. Besides, one will not be permitted to love even life more than God.

Chapter XV.

Now, then, the epistles of the apostles also are well known. And do we, (you say), in all respects guileless souls and doves merely, love to go astray? I should think from eagerness to live. But let it be so, that meaning departs from their epistles. And yet, that the apostles endured such sufferings, we know: the teaching is clear. This only I perceive in running through the Acts. I am not at all on the search. The prisons there, and the bonds, and the scourges, and the big stones, and the swords, and the onsets by the Jews, and the assemblies of the heathen, and the indictments by tribunes, and the hearing of causes by kings, and the judgment-seats of proconsuls and the name of Cæsar, do not need an interpreter. That Peter is struck, that Stephen is overwhelmed by stones, that James is slain as is a victim at the altar, that Paul is beheaded has been written in their own blood. And if a heretic wishes his confidence to rest upon a public record, the archives of the empire will speak, as would the stones of Jerusalem. We read the lives of the Cæsars: At Rome Nero was the first who stained with blood the rising faith. Then is Peter girt by another, when he is made fast to the cross. Then does Paul obtain a birth suited to Roman citizenship, when in Rome he springs to life again ennobled by martyrdom. Wherever I read of these occurrences, so soon as I do so, I learn to suffer; nor does it signify to me which I follow as teachers of martyrdom, whether the declarations or the deaths of the apostles, save that in their deaths I recall their declarations also. For they would not have suffered ought of a kind they had not previously known they had to suffer. When Agabus, making use of corresponding action too, had foretold that bonds awaited Paul, the disciples, weeping and entreating that he would not venture upon going to Jerusalem, entreated in vain. As for him, having a mind to illustrate what he had always taught, he says, "Why weep ye, and grieve my heart? But for my part, I could wish not only to suffer bonds, but also to die at Jerusalem, for the name of my Lord Jesus Christ." And so they yielded by saying, "Let the will of the Lord be done;" feeling sure, doubtless, that sufferings are included in the will of God. For they had tried to keep him back with the intention not of dissuading, but to show love for him; as yearning for (the preservation of) the apostle, not as counselling against martyrdom. And if even then a Prodicus or Valentinus stood by, suggesting that one must not confess on the earth before men, and must do so the less in truth, that God may not (seem to) thirst for blood, and Christ for a repayment of suffering, as though He besought it with the view of obtaining salvation by it for Himself also, he would have immediately heard from the servant of God what the devil had from the Lord: "Get thee behind me, Satan; thou art an offence unto me. It is written, Thou shalt worship the Lord thy God, and Him only shalt thou serve." But even now it will be right that he hears it, seeing that, long after, he has poured forth these poisons, which not even thus are to injure readily any of the weak ones, if any one in faith will drink, before being hurt, or even immediately after, this draught of ours.

www.ingramcontent.com/pod-product-compliance
Lightning Source LLC
Chambersburg PA
CBHW052044070526
44584CB00018B/2603